MW01114083

ISBN-13: 978-1493615193
ISBN-10: 149361519X

All Bible references used are from the KJV unless otherwise stated. The 1611 edition of the King James Version (KJV) is in the public domain.

What Must I Do To Be Saved?

How many times have we heard these words across our Land? How many opinions do we have in regards to this subject? Jesus said, in Matt. 16:16, Upon this Rock I will build my church and the gates of Hell shall not prevail against it. Jesus said he would build HIS CHURCH.

The bible says in Ephesians 1: 22-23 that Christ is the head over all things to the church (not a church) which is his Body. Ephesians 4:4 says, there is one body and one spirit even as you are called in one Hope of your calling. 1 Corinthians 12:13 says for by one spirit are we all baptized into one body, whether we be Jew or Gentiles, whether we be bond or free; and have been all made to drink into one spirit.

In 1 Corinthians 12:27 the Apostle Paul said, now ye are the body of Christ, and members in particular. In Galatians 1:6-7 he spoke, "I marvel that ye are so soon removed from Him that called you into the Grace of Christ unto another Gospel which is not another". In Romans 1:16-17, Paul said, "For I am not ashamed of the Gospel of Jesus Christ: for it is the Power of God unto salvation to everyone that believeth: to the Jew first, and also to the Greek. For therein is the righteousness of God revealed from faith to faith: as it is written, The Just shall live by faith".

So, for us to receive salvation and the righteousness of God, we must hear the Gospel of Jesus Christ. Because Jesus said, the words I speak are spirit and life. So what did Jesus preach?

For this reason, this study has been put together for your benefit. If we could remove all of the labels or name brands out of our mind for a while, such as Pentecostal, Church of Christ, Church of God, Nazarene, Baptist, Methodist etc....; sit down with the Bible and see what was the Gospel of Jesus Christ. In II Corinthians 13:5, the Apostle Paul said, "Examine yourselves, whether ye be in the faith; prove your own selves. Know ye not your own selves, how that Jesus Christ is in you, except ye be reprobates? Ephesians 4:5 says, "One Lord, One Faith, One baptism". (not church group or Denominations but one Gospel)

Who would you Believe to tell you how to be SAVED?

How about the LORD JESUS CHRIST?

So often we hear so much about what people think about being saved that we pay very little attention to what Jesus said. With careful examination let us study the word of God and see what Jesus said about being saved.

When we study the word of God, there is only one who can speak on this subject of salvation, that is Jesus The Christ.

1. Jesus said in John 6:63-64
It is the spirit that quickeneth; the flesh profiteth nothing: the words that I speak unto you, they are spirit, and they are life. But there are some of you that believe not. For Jesus knew from the beginning who they were that believed not, and who should betray him.

2. Hebrews 12:2

Looking unto Jesus the author and finisher of our faith; who for the joy that was set before him endured the cross, despising the shame, and is set down at the right hand of the throne of God.

3. Acts 2:36

Therefore let all the house of Israel know assuredly, that God hath made that same Jesus, whom ye have crucified, both Lord and Christ.

4. John 6:68

Then Simon Peter answered him, Lord, to whom shall we go? thou hast the words of eternal life.

5. Jesus said in John 14:6

Jesus saith unto him, I am the way, the truth, and the life: no man cometh unto the Father, but by me.

6. Colossians 2:8-10

Beware lest any man spoil you through philosophy and vain deceit, after the tradition of men, after the rudiments of the world, and not after Christ. For in him dwelleth all the fulness of the Godhead bodily. And ye are complete in him, which is the head of all principality and power:

7. 1 Timothy 6:3-5

If any man teach otherwise, and consent not to wholesome words, even the words of our Lord Jesus Christ, and to the doctrine which is according to godliness; He is proud, knowing nothing, but doting about questions and strifes of words, whereof cometh envy, strife, railings, evil surmisings, Perverse disputings of men of corrupt minds, and destitute of the truth, supposing that gain is godliness: from such withdraw thyself.

8. **Jesus said in John 10:7-9**

   Then said Jesus unto them again, Verily, verily, I say unto you, I am the door of the sheep. All that ever came before me are thieves and robbers: but the sheep did not hear them. I am the door: by me if any man enter in, he shall be saved, and shall go in and out, and find pasture.

9. **Acts 3:22-23**

   For Moses truly said unto the fathers, A prophet shall the Lord your God raise up unto you of your brethren, like unto me; him shall ye hear in all things whatsoever he shall say unto you. And it shall come to pass, that every soul, which will not hear that prophet, shall be destroyed from among the people.

So! What Jesus says is important concerning being saved.

10. **Jesus said in Matthew 16:18**

   ...I will build my church; and the gates of hell shall not prevail against it.

Jesus is the contractor. You and I are just labourer's together. He is the Boss.

He is the head. We are the body. Jesus is the only one in the Bible who ever had a church. which is his body. Why do we become members of other men's churches? Such as Baptist, Methodist, Catholic, Presbyterian, Pentecostal, Church of God, Assemblies of God, Church of Christ, Lutheran, Nazarene, etc..

11. When Jesus said in Mark 16:16

He that believeth and is baptized shall be saved; but he that believeth not shall be damned.

Did He know what He was saying?

12. John 1:17

For the law was given by Moses, but grace and truth came by Jesus Christ.

13. Mark 12:14

And when they were come, they say unto him, Master, we know that thou art true, and carest for no man: for thou regardest not the person of men, but teachest the way of God in truth: Is it lawful to give tribute to Caesar, or not?

When Jesus said, ye must believe and be baptized in Mark 16:16, we must study to find out what he is telling us.

Must Believe..... Must Believe What?

14. Hebrews 11:6

But without faith it is impossible to please him: for he that cometh to God must believe that he is, and that he is a rewarder of them that diligently seek him.

15. John 8:24

I said therefore unto you, that ye shall die in your sins: for if ye believe not that I am he, ye shall die in your sins.

Before, Jesus said, no man cometh unto the Father except by me.

16. 1 John 2:23
Whosoever denieth the Son, the same hath not the Father: (but) he that acknowledgeth the Son hath the Father also.

17. Jesus said Luke 13: 3 & 5
I tell you, Nay: but, except ye repent, ye shall all likewise perish.
I tell you, Nay: but, except ye repent, ye shall all likewise perish.

18. Mark 1:15
And saying, The time is fulfilled, and the kingdom of God is at hand: repent ye, and believe the gospel.

19. Romans 1:16-17
For I am not ashamed of the gospel of Christ: for it is the power of God unto salvation to every one that believeth; to the Jew first, and also to the Greek. For therein is the righteousness of God revealed from faith to faith: as it is written, The just shall live by faith.

20. Jesus said John 7:38-40
He that believeth on me, as the scripture hath said, out of his belly shall flow rivers of living water. (But this spake he of the Spirit, which they that believe on him should receive: for the Holy Ghost was not yet given; because that Jesus was not yet glorified.) Many of the people therefore, when they heard this saying, said, Of a truth this is the Prophet.

Jesus said, ye must believe I am the way, the Truth, the Life, the Door. No one can be saved any other way, except by the words Jesus said.

21. Jesus said: John 3: 3 & 5
Jesus answered and said unto him, Verily, verily, I say unto thee, Except a man be born again, he cannot see the kingdom of God.
Jesus answered, Verily, verily, I say unto thee, Except a man be born of water and of the Spirit, he cannot enter into the kingdom of God.

What Jesus said in Mark 16-16, he that believeth and is baptized shall be saved, but he that believeth not shall be damned.

Now that we have studied and found what we have to believe, How do we Baptize?

For the Bible says there is one Lord, one Faith, and one Baptism. He said, he that believeth and is Baptized shall be saved.

22. Jesus said: Matthew 28: 19-20
Go ye therefore, and teach all nations, baptizing them in the name of the Father, and of the Son, and of the Holy Ghost: Teaching them to observe all things whatsoever I have commanded you: and, lo, I am with you alway, even unto the end of the world. Amen.

23. Jesus said : Mark 16:16
He that believeth and is baptized shall be saved; but he that believeth not shall be damned.

24. Jesus said: Luke 24:47
And that repentance and remission of sins should be preached in his name among all nations, beginning at Jerusalem.

25. Jesus said : John 3:5
Jesus answered, Verily, verily, I say unto thee, Except a man be born of water and of the Spirit, he cannot enter into the kingdom of God.

When Peter preached in Acts 2, the people cried out "what must we do"?

26. Acts 2:38
Then Peter said unto them, Repent, and be baptized every one of you in the name of Jesus Christ for the remission of sins, and ye shall receive the gift of the Holy Ghost.

Why did Peter preach Baptism in the Name of Jesus?

1) Luke 24:47......Because Jesus said, in my name beginning at Jerusalem .

2) Matthew 16:18.... Because Jesus said, , I will Build my church.

3) Matthew 16:19.... Jesus said unto Peter, I will give you the keys of the kingdom, and whatsoever thou shalt bind on earth shall be bound in heaven and what so ever thou shall loose on earth shall be loosed in heaven.

Jesus said in the Name of the Father. Jesus said in John 5:43, I come in my Father's name.

27. Hebrews 1:4
Being made so much better than the angels, as he hath by
inheritance obtained a more excellent name than they.

28. Philippians 2:9-10
Wherefore God also hath highly exalted him, and given
him a name which is above every name: That at the
name of Jesus every knee should bow, of things in
heaven, and things in earth, and things under the earth;

When Jesus said in the Name of the Father He meant in the name of the Father.

What is the Fathers Name?

> ➤ John 5:43 Jesus said it was his name.

> ➤ John 17:6 I have manifested thy name unto the men which thou gavest me.

> ➤ John 17:11 Keep in thy name.

> ➤ John 17:12 I have kept them in thy name.

> ➤ John 17:26 I have declared thy name.

> ➤ John 10:25 The works I do in my fathers name they bear witness of me.

> ➤ John 12:23-28 Father glorify thy name.

Jesus said in the name of the Father.
The Father's name is Jesus. (John 5:43)

Name of the Son?
The Son's name is Jesus. (Matthew 1:21-25)

Name of the Holy Ghost?
The name of the Holy Ghost is Jesus. (John 14:26)

In I Cor. 1:10-15, the Apostle Paul asked a question. Why are there divisions among you? Some say I am of Paul, and I am of Apollos, and I am of Cephas and I am of Christ. Is Christ divided?

Let me put it this way. We say "I am Pentecostal, I am Baptist, I am Church of Christ, I am Church of God etc..."

Is Christ Divided?

Was Paul crucified for you? Were you baptized in the name of Paul? No! You get baptized in the name of the one who died for you. Why? you ask. Because:

29. Romans 6:3
Know ye not, that so many of us as were baptized into Jesus Christ were baptized into his death?

30. Galatians 3:27
For as many of you as have been baptized into Christ have put on Christ.

31. Romans 8:1
There is therefore now no condemnation to them which are in Christ Jesus, who walk not after the flesh, but after the Spirit.

32. Colossians 3: 2-3
Set your affection on things above, not on things on the earth. For ye are dead, and your life is hid with Christ in God.

Why is Baptism so important?

1) Acts 2:38 Because it is for the remission of sins.

2) Acts 22:16 Washes away our sins.

3) Col. 2:11-12 We are circumcised and put off the Body of sin.

4) Col. 2:14 Blots out sin.

5) Prov. 18:10 The Name of the Lord = Safety.

33. Acts 9:5
And he said, Who art thou, Lord? And the Lord said, I am Jesus whom thou persecutest: it is hard for thee to kick against the pricks.

34. Acts 2:37
Now when they heard this, they were pricked in their heart, and said unto Peter and to the rest of the apostles, Men and brethren, what shall we do?

35. Acts 2:36
Therefore let all the house of Israel know assuredly, that God hath made that same Jesus, whom ye have crucified, both Lord and Christ.

The name of the Lord is Jesus.

Why is it so Important to baptize in the name of Jesus?

1) Jesus said to. Luke 24:47

2) Peter who had the keys to the kingdom said to. Acts 2:38

3) The Apostles preached in the name of Jesus.

4) Neither is there salvation in any other. Acts 4:12

5) Whatsoever ye do in word or deed, do all in the name of Jesus, giving thanks to God and the Father by him. Col. 3: 17

6) For ye are washed sanctified and justified by the name. 1 Cor 6:11

7) The whole family is named in Heaven and Earth. Eph 3:14-15

8) Then they that gladly received his words were baptized and the same day there were added unto them about three thousand souls.

There is one Family of God and one Family name. Jesus.

➢ The whole family is named in Heaven and Earth. Eph 3:14-15

➢ Jesus said I call my sheep by name. John 10:3

➢ If my people which are called by my name shall humble themselves. 2 Chron 7:14

➢ And they shall put my name upon the children of Israel and I will bless them. Numbers 6:22-27

36. Jesus said : Matthew 24:9
Then shall they deliver you up to be afflicted, and shall kill you: and ye shall be hated of all nations for my name's sake.

37. Acts 4:18
And they called them, and commanded them not to speak at all nor teach in the name of Jesus.

- ➢ In Acts 2
  - = The early church baptized in the name of Jesus.
- ➢ In Acts 8
  - = The Samaritans were baptized in the name of Jesus.
- ➢ In Acts 10
  - = The Gentiles were baptized in the name of Jesus.
- ➢ In Acts 17
  - = The Disciples of John were rebaptized in the name of Jesus Christ.

So what doeth hinder you? Arise and be baptized washing away your sins calling on the name of the Lord Jesus Christ.

Is the Holy Ghost Necessary?

38. Jesus said John 3:5

Jesus answered, Verily, verily, I say unto thee, Except a man be born of water and of the Spirit, he cannot enter into the kingdom of God.

39. Hebrews 6:1-3

Therefore leaving the principles of the doctrine of Christ, let us go on unto perfection; not laying again the foundation of repentance from dead works, and of faith toward God, Of the doctrine of baptisms, and of laying on of hands, and of resurrection of the dead, and of eternal judgment. And this will we do, if God permit.

40. Paul said Romans 8:9

But ye are not in the flesh, but in the Spirit, if so be that the Spirit of God dwell in you. Now if any man have not the Spirit of Christ, he is none of his.

What Spirit did Christ have?

- ➢ Matt 4:1 Jesus was led of the Spirit.

- ➢ Luke 4:1 Jesus being full of the Holy Ghost.

- ➢ Luke 4:14 Jesus returned in power of Spirit.

- ➢ Eph 4:4 There is one Body and one Spirit even as ye are called in one Hope of your calling.

41. Jesus said : John 4: 24
God is a Spirit: and they that worship him must worship him in spirit and in truth.

42. God said: Isaiah 28:11-12
For with stammering lips and another tongue will he speak to this people. To whom he said, This is the rest wherewith ye may cause the weary to rest; and this is the refreshing: yet they would not hear.

43. Hebrews 4:11
Let us labour therefore to enter into that rest, lest any man fall after the same example of unbelief.

44. Matthew 3:11
I indeed baptize you with water unto repentance: but he that cometh after me is mightier than I, whose shoes I am not worthy to bear: he shall baptize you with the Holy Ghost, and with fire:

45. Jesus said : John 7:37-39
In the last day, that great day of the feast, Jesus stood and cried, saying, If any man thirst, let him come unto me, and drink. He that believeth on me, as the scripture hath said, out of his belly shall flow rivers of living water. (But this spake he of the Spirit, which they that believe on him should receive: for the Holy Ghost was not yet given; because that Jesus was not yet glorified.)

46. Jesus said : John 14:16

And I will pray the Father, and he shall give you another Comforter, that he may abide with you for ever;

47. Jesus said : John 14:26

But the Comforter, which is the Holy Ghost, whom the Father will send in my name, he shall teach you all things, and bring all things to your remembrance, whatsoever I have said unto you.

48. Jesus said : Luke 24:49

And, behold, I send the promise of my Father upon you: but tarry ye in the city of Jerusalem, until ye be endued with power from on high.

49. Jesus said : John 20:22

And when he had said this, he breathed on them, and saith unto them, Receive ye the Holy Ghost:

50. Jesus said : Acts 1:4-5

And, being assembled together with them, commanded them that they should not depart from Jerusalem, but wait for the promise of the Father, which, saith he, ye have heard of me. For John truly baptized with water; but ye shall be baptized with the Holy Ghost not many days hence.

51. Jesus said : Luke 11:13

If ye then, being evil, know how to give good gifts unto your children: how much more shall your heavenly Father give the Holy Spirit to them that ask him?

52. Acts 2:17

And it shall come to pass in the last days, saith God, I will pour out of my Spirit upon all flesh: and your sons and your daughters shall prophesy, and your young men shall see visions, and your old men shall dream dreams:

53. Acts 2:38
Then Peter said unto them, Repent, and be baptized every one of you in the name of Jesus Christ for the remission of sins, and ye shall receive the gift of the Holy Ghost.

54. Acts 2:39
For the promise is unto you, and to your children, and to all that are afar off, even as many as the Lord our God shall call.

Why is the Spirit necessary?

1) I Cor. 12:13 By one spirit we are all baptized into one body.
2) Rom. 8: 13 We do mortify the deeds of the body.
3) Rom. 8:16 The spirit beareth witness with our spirit.
4) Rom. 8:26 The spirit helpeth our infirmities. It maketh intercession.
5) Rom. 8: 11 The spirit will quicken our mortal bodies IF it dwells in us.

55. Ephesians 4:4
There is one body, and one Spirit, even as ye are called in one hope of your calling;

So, when you are told, believe on the Lord Jesus Christ and thou shalt be saved, be careful lest men spoil you.

56. Colossians 2:8-10
Beware lest any man spoil you through philosophy and vain deceit, after the tradition of men, after the rudiments of the world, and not after Christ. For in him dwelleth all the fulness of the Godhead bodily. And ye are complete in him, which is the head of all principality and power:

The Bible says there is a way to be saved. Notice what you just read! A way to be saved, NOT WAYS to be saved.

57. Jesus said : John 14:6
Jesus saith unto him, I am the way, the truth, and the life: no man cometh unto the Father, but by me.

58. Jesus said : John 10:7
Then said Jesus unto them again, Verily, verily, I say unto you, I am the door of the sheep.

59. Jesus said : John 10:9
I am the door: by me if any man enter in, he shall be saved, and shall go in and out, and find pasture.

60. Jesus called his disciples in : Luke 6:12-13
And it came to pass in those days, that he went out into a mountain to pray, and continued all night in prayer to God.   And when it was day, he called unto him his disciples: and of them he chose twelve, whom also he named apostles;

61. Jesus said : John 17:8
For I have given unto them the words which thou gavest me; and they have received them, and have known surely that I came out from thee, and they have believed that thou didst send me.

62. The Apostle Paul said : Ephesians 2:19-22
Now therefore ye are no more strangers and foreigners, but fellowcitizens with the saints, and of the household of God;   And are built upon the foundation of the apostles and prophets, Jesus Christ himself being the chief corner stone;   In whom all the building fitly framed together groweth unto an holy temple in the Lord: In whom ye also are builded together for an habitation of God through the Spirit.

63. Paul said : I Corinthians 3:9-11

For we are labourers together with God: ye are God's husbandry, ye are God's building. According to the grace of God which is given unto me, as a wise masterbuilder, I have laid the foundation, and another buildeth thereon. But let every man take heed how he buildeth thereupon. For other foundation can no man lay than that is laid, which is Jesus Christ.

64. Paul said : Hebrews 6:1-3

Therefore leaving the principles of the doctrine of Christ, let us go on unto perfection; not laying again the foundation of repentance from dead works, and of faith toward God, Of the doctrine of baptisms, and of laying on of hands, and of resurrection of the dead, and of eternal judgment. And this will we do, if God permit.

65. Paul said : I Timothy 6:3-5

If any man teach otherwise, and consent not to wholesome words, even the words of our Lord Jesus Christ, and to the doctrine which is according to godliness; He is proud, knowing nothing, but doting about questions and strifes of words, whereof cometh envy, strife, railings, evil surmisings, Perverse disputings of men of corrupt minds, and destitute of the truth, supposing that gain is godliness: from such withdraw thyself.

66. Jude 3-5

Beloved, when I gave all diligence to write unto you of the common salvation, it was needful for me to write unto you, and exhort you that ye should earnestly contend for the faith which was once delivered unto the saints. For there are certain men crept in unawares, who were before of old ordained to this condemnation, ungodly men, turning the grace of our God into lasciviousness, and denying the only Lord God, and our Lord Jesus Christ. I will therefore put you in remembrance, though ye once knew this, how that the Lord, having saved the people out of the land of Egypt, afterward destroyed them that believed not.

Earnestly contend for THE FAITH.

Not a faith.

67. II Corinthians 13:5

Examine yourselves, whether ye be in the faith; prove your own selves. Know ye not your own selves, how that Jesus Christ is in you, except ye be reprobates?

The word FAITH in Jude 3-5 and in I Cor13:5 is the same Greek word pistis (pis'-tis) which means persuasion, i.e. credence; moral conviction (of religious truth, or the truthfulness of God or a religious teacher), especially reliance upon Christ for salvation; abstractly, constancy in such profession; by extension, the system of religious (Gospel) truth itself: KJV-- assurance, belief, believe, faith, fidelity.

68. Proverbs. 14:12 & 16:25

There is a way which seemeth right unto a man, but the end thereof are the ways of death.
There is a way that seemeth right unto a man, but the end thereof are the ways of death.

We know there are times when entire churches have embraced a gospel that was not of God. In Galatians 1:6-9 Paul rebukes the church because it had turned to another gospel

69. Galatians 1:6-9

I marvel that ye are so soon removed from him that called you into the grace of Christ unto another gospel: Which is not another; but there be some that trouble you, and would pervert the gospel of Christ. But though we, or an angel from heaven, preach any other gospel unto you than that which we have preached unto you, let him be accursed. As we said before, so say I now again, If any man preach any other gospel unto you than that ye have received, let him be accursed.

We know that churches have embraced doctrines which God does not approve of such as Revelation chapter 2 and 3. He commanded 5 out of 7 churches to repent. How very tragic it would be to embrace a doctrine in which Christ did not approve of and be lost. So many times we can embrace doctrines which Christ did not approve of and can be lost. We can be sincerely wrong in our belief. That is why the Apostle Paul said Examine yourselves. (I Cor. 13:5)

70. Paul said : Romans 2:16
In the day when God shall judge the secrets of men by Jesus Christ according to my gospel.

Paul said that God would judge the world by HIS gospel. Why? Because he received HIS gospel from the Lord Jesus Christ Himself.

71. Galatians 1: 11-12
But I certify you, brethren, that the gospel which was preached of me is not after man. For I neither received it of man, neither was I taught it, but by the revelation of Jesus Christ.

72. Galatians 1:15-19
But when it pleased God, who separated me from my mother's womb, and called me by his grace, To reveal his Son in me, that I might preach him among the heathen; immediately I conferred not with flesh and

blood: Neither went I up to Jerusalem to them which were apostles before me; but I went into Arabia, and returned again unto Damascus.   Then after three years I went up to Jerusalem to see Peter, and abode with him fifteen days.   But other of the apostles saw I none, save James the Lord's brother.

Paul went to Jerusalem to see Peter. Why? To confirm that he (Paul) was preaching the same gospel as Peter had preached in Jerusalem , since Peter having received the keys to the kingdom from Jesus Christ himself. Matt 16:19

73. Paul said : Galatians 2:1-2
Then fourteen years after I went up again to Jerusalem with Barnabas, and took Titus with me also.   And I went up by revelation, and communicated unto them that gospel which I preach among the Gentiles, but privately to them which were of reputation, lest by any means I should run, or had run, in vain.

Peter looked at some people in the 4th chapter of Acts and said, this is the stone ye "builders" have set at naught. There are a lot of big church "builders", organization "builders", congregation "builders" who pay no attention to the Chief Cornerstone.

Again, please let me stress that Jesus said (in John 10:63-64) the words that I speak are Spirit and they are life.

Please, let me stress again the importance of what Paul instructed Timothy.

74. Paul told Timothy : I Timothy 6:3-5

If any man teach otherwise, and consent not to wholesome words, even the words of our Lord Jesus Christ, and to the doctrine which is according to godliness; He is proud, knowing nothing, but doting about questions and strifes of words, whereof cometh envy, strife, railings, evil surmisings, Perverse disputings of men of corrupt minds, and destitute of the truth, supposing that gain is godliness: from such withdraw thyself.

75. Jesus said : John 12:47-48

And if any man hear my words, and believe not, I judge him not: for I came not to judge the world, but to save the world. He that rejecteth me, and receiveth not my words, hath one that judgeth him: the word that I have spoken, the same shall judge him in the last day.

I ask you to please look at the word of God and examine yourself before it is too late to do something about what you believe.

76. II Thessalonians 2:10-12

And with all deceivableness of unrighteousness in them that perish; because they received not the love of the truth, that they might be saved. And for this cause God shall send them strong delusion, that they should believe a lie: That they all might be damned who believed not the truth, but had pleasure in unrighteousness.

77. Acts 18:24-26

And a certain Jew named Apollos, born at Alexandria, an eloquent man, and mighty in the scriptures, came to Ephesus. This man was instructed in the way of the Lord; and being fervent in the spirit, he spake and taught diligently the things of the Lord, knowing only the baptism of John. And he began to speak boldly in the synagogue: whom when Aquila and Priscilla had heard, they took him unto them, and expounded unto him the way of God more perfectly.

23

Apollos was eloquent man and mighty in the scripture, but he only knew the baptism of John. Priscilla and Aquila expounded the way more perfectly to him. We must be saved at any cost.

I have not written this Bible Study to offend or to get you to join the church that I Pastor. I have put this Bible Study together because this is what the Bible teaches about being saved or being born again as Jesus said in John 3:3.

I ask you this question, have you been born again of water and the spirit? If not, please Repent and be Baptized in the name of Jesus Christ for the remission of your sins and ye shall receive the gift of the Holy Ghost (Acts 2:38) with the evidence of speaking with other tongues, as the spirit gives the utterance. (Acts 2:4)

78. Acts 10:44-48

> While Peter yet spake these words, the Holy Ghost fell on all them which heard the word. And they of the circumcision which believed were astonished, as many as came with Peter, because that on the Gentiles also was poured out the gift of the Holy Ghost. For they heard them speak with tongues, and magnify God. Then answered Peter, Can any man forbid water, that these should not be baptized, which have received the Holy Ghost as well as we? And he commanded them to be baptized in the name of the Lord. Then prayed they him to tarry certain days.

Notice in the scripture, there are those who received the Holy Ghost before they were baptized. Peter commanded them to be baptized in Jesus name.

There are those in Acts 19, who were believers, who had not received the Holy Ghost, who were rebaptized and then received the Holy Ghost and spoke with tongues.

If you will obey the gospel in YOUR Bible, you will know what it means to be born again of water and of the spirit as mentioned in I Peter 1:19-23.

79. I Peter 1:19-23

But with the precious blood of Christ, as of a lamb without blemish and without spot: Who verily was foreordained before the foundation of the world, but was manifest in these last times for you,   Who by him do believe in God, that raised him up from the dead, and gave him glory; that your faith and hope might be in God. Seeing ye have purified your souls in obeying the truth through the Spirit unto unfeigned love of the brethren, see that ye love one another with a pure heart fervently: Being born again, not of corruptible seed, but of incorruptible, by the word of God, which liveth and abideth for ever.

80. Hebrews 2:1-4

Therefore we ought to give the more earnest heed to the things which we have heard, lest at any time we should let them slip.   For if the word spoken by angels was stedfast, and every transgression and disobedience received a just recompence of reward;   How shall we escape, if we neglect so great salvation; which at the first began to be spoken by the Lord, and was confirmed unto us by them that heard him;   God also bearing them witness, both with signs and wonders, and with divers miracles, and gifts of the Holy Ghost, according to his own will?

Paul told Timothy in I Timothy 4:16 take heed unto thyself, and unto the doctrine; continue in them: for in doing this thou shalt both save thyself, and them that hear thee. PLEASE examine yourself and your doctrine. The most important thing in this world is to save our soul! Peter said in Acts 2:40, "SAVE YOURSELVES".

Your Servant in Christ Jesus,
Bishop Jack B. Batson

Made in the USA
Middletown, DE
07 October 2022

12214853R00015